Looking Through Letterboxes

CAROLINE BIRD was born in London. She has lived in Leeds for most of her life, but now lives in South London. She is currently studying for her GCSEs. She was a winner of the Simon Elvin Young Poet of the Year Awards in 1999 and 2000. Her poems have been published in *PN Review* and other journals. This is her first collection.

:

CAROLINE BIRD

Looking Through Letterboxes

CARCANET

First published in Great Britain in 2002 by
Carcanet Press Limited
Alliance House
30 Cross Street
Manchester M2 7AQ

A CIP catalogue record for this book
is available from the British Library

ISBN 1 85754 590 7

The publisher acknowledges financial assistance
from the Arts Council of England

Set in Monotype Garamond by XL Publishing Services, Tiverton
Printed and bound in England by SRP Ltd, Exeter

Contents

Dusk and Petrol

If you cross your eyes slightly then the lawn is on fire.
I watch a plane flying low, flaring through the dusk.
I stir my coffee twice and wait for it to settle
as the man on the radio with a voice like sinking bread
tells the nation that dousing yourself in petrol
isn't a good thing to do. Spontaneous rainfalls of rolling eyes
are swooping across the country, they see everything,
so don't go out of the house, don't stay in the house,
don't move, run for your life. My coffee is too hot,
I now have a mouth like the bottom of a steaming pipe
and it's too early to go to bed. I think about hospitals
to pass the time, think about memories seeping through scars,
think about fainting surgeons.
'The doctors said there was nothing they could do.'
Why do we have doctors that can't do anything?
Can they walk, talk, keep a clean house?
The lawn is burning itself out now, I pick up the phone
then put it down, repeat the action. Love
is a double-bladed knife. I find it much easier to make enemies,
I can make them out of gingerbread, playdoh, leaves,
I can model them to look like you.
I can place them face-down in the sink.

A Window Overlooking a Garden

Only takes you so far, fate. Dropped me at your door
with a fist poised to knock.
People leave holes behind them, now I fly
to avoid the ground. I opened a small wooden box,
the past hit me in the neck like a truncheon,
a magic roundabout somewhere changed direction.

On my way to you, walking through your city
late in the moon/sun swap. Neon with its glare
and all the high-heeled glory of drunken women,
running from nothing.

The city unravelled itself to follow me across the lawn
and down by the stone boy who was coughing
transparent blood. The flowers were dying for winter,
the wind was whipped,
love rolled off my tongue and into the night.

Only takes you so far, fate. To the end of the pier
but not into the lake, to the mouth but not the smile.
The city is catching me up now, it's black breath on my hair,
I watch as my fist is unclenched,
my footsteps taken backwards and erased,

somewhere a window laughs.

Umbrella

No surprise to me as the headmaster
leaps out from an icing covered bomb
and gives me my cake, tells me to eat it, fast

as the minutes are passing
and they're pissing against the graffiti in the toilets,
someone has scrawled my name,

someone has sold my laughter lines
for a sniff of freedom, thrown all my chances
at the dart board, made another bull's-eye blind.

Well let me tell you that it's all whistled away
like a slow fire-work over my head,
and I've got enough on my plate, what with exams

and false starts and questions and more questions,
a riddle recited in assembly instead of a prayer.
I go up the chimney down, what am I?

An umbrella.

I bow my head,
hold tight to my riddle book.

The Song You Left Behind

You give me recurring dreams.
The yawn, mumble of sleep before you slept,
the stretching, sighing sounds
still ring in my ears like an unanswered phone.
I have kept a thread of hair, a drop of ink,
your drinking flask. I sip herbal tea, then spit it,
hot and scented, from the sky-light.
Don't ask me why. The windows smear
with strangers, the apples rot on trees
and the man next-door shovels soil from the front
to the back garden, from the back to the front
and nothing ever grows.

Last night the devil
behind my eyelids
put a gun to your cheek
and bundled you
like dirty washing into his car.
Your blood on the leather.
Gold-ringed fingers over your eyes.
I was in the back seat
and would have saved you,
had it been my name
your lips were screaming.
The pounding of crimson
windscreen wipers,
your beautiful bleeding mouth.
I awoke,
shaking, biting the pillow.

Now your face is my face. I'm beginning to hate
the mirror for the way it leaps at me
from the corner of the room, a spitting image.
Each morning your smile beams
through my mouth and your throaty laugh
plays havoc on my tonsils. I cut my hair,
hoard stolen smiles, practise
sitting without first looking down.
I sing with you every night, alone,
my own ventriloquist, my own dummy.

It sounds strange. It is. I can feel the dream
creeping up my veins, I can feel a smoothness
in my skin that was not there before.

I record our song on tape, but it sounds better live.
The harmonies are glorious, the low notes
make craters and the high notes raise sparks.

I wake, brimming like a storm
and your voice rises up from my stomach,
beats at the cage of my tongue until we boom
out over the rooftops, until we resound
down every chimney, halt the spade
of the man next-door, crash
into every living room, break the walls
of every kitchen and seep, finally,
onto the window-sills,
to devour every cooling apple-pie.

Except no one cools their pies on window-sills any more.

But if they did.
If they did, our song would be in there like a shot,
turning the apple into acid, the pastry into gold,
churning, contaminating, making everything
poisonous and precious.

Owl Poem

I refuse to write about an owl,
better to write about a person with an owl,
or a person who wants an owl, or better still,
a person who hates owls and will never
have an owl.

Spilt Milk

There's things I wish I didn't know, arms I'd like to rock you with.
But my stomach is a marble and I think I might break.

Outside the small blue windows, the clouds are open.
And what I meant to say was, if you ever want to talk.
But I stood in my room for an hour last night,
                                        just swaying on my heels
and there's things I wish I didn't know,
arms I'd like to catch you with.

You make me laugh so hard, I never would have known
the river behind the beaches of your eyes.
And there's things I wish I didn't know, arms that fail me every time.

And there's moments I have kept from you, if you ever want to talk,
moments that make no sense to me. Like why, after breakfast,
alone in the house, did I spill the milk then cry over the stain?

And why did I soak it up gently with a sponge,
call it by your name?
And why was I so sure that you had melted?

Bad Weather

You were the drowning rat
and I was the shivering
cartoon cloud
directly above your head.
And when you greeted me,
with your transparent top
and dripping scowl,
to say 'It was sunny
before you came,'
it was purely for your sake
that I turned around
and got back on the train.

No One in the Waiting Room Looks Up

A power-ranger child runs up the wall. Which wall?
The white wall, the one which gives you a coma

if you stare for too long. The child doesn't come down,
ate so much chocolate from the vending machines,

he's learnt how to fly. But no one in the waiting room looks up.
Christmas is coming and Santa Claus is in Ward 17,

turn left at the end of the corridor. A woman with a pick-axe
is strolling past the operation room, looking for someone to whack.

A prune-faced man is spray-painting obscenities
up and down the hall and a dressing-gown awash in antiseptic

swaggers around the hospital, proud of its bodylessness.
A patient in a wheelbarrow is sped across the corridor,

choking to death on a grape – though of course they will say
he choked until he was un-alive, but not dead,

because people don't die. Not even the lad who's still up the wall,
which wall? The white wall. But no one in the waiting room looks up.

Disappear

Staring at you for too long, tracing your face,
remembering the stone through the sweet shop window.
Glass spitting teeth.
Laid out, wide open rows of *stain your tongues,*
stick to your gums, jam down your throats
and melt in your mouths.
It was like that when I touched your cheek
and thought I sensed
the twang and echo of the alarm.

Your hands were searching spider joints, your hair,
syrup running down your face, your eyes
in the scoop of the dark
as you smiled slow,
stretched just right, squeezed your fingers
slightly round the curve of my heart,
where you knew it hurt.
I lay in the groove of your leg,
knowing you'd be gone
when the light shattered on the midnight sky.
But I didn't believe it, I was sure
I could twist the knife forever and you'd still be
waiting by the phone box,
waiting by the corner shop,
waiting at the traffic lights,
waiting underground.

Now you're lying low somewhere,
your back to the wall
with too many smoking shot-guns to know who's to blame.
Even now I can see you, dropping your head,
talking this and that,
forgetting about the other.
I know the thought waves in this pale air,
you're speaking memories,
you're swallowing the truth.

But I'm still here
looking out of the window at the empty road,
thinking of the time when I disappeared.
When I left the sweets and legged it,
away from the throbbing sirens
and the screaming pound of my chest.
Instead of taking my time,
picking the ripest sugars from the plastic jars
and strolling out the back into the alley.

Pissed Off Phone Box

Master of the ring back,
phone box, not phone booth,

I bug people's private life,
you wouldn't believe.

At night you get the rough ones,
the 'urgently need to phone,

left the kettle on' vandals
who thump my windows to be let in,

once in, complain
about the draught. Hoodlums

scrawling their latest love
in the yellow pages of my favourite book.

In bad areas I've heard of smashes
but that only happens to other phone boxes,

not round here they don't.
Two o'clock in the morning's worst,

I sometimes swing my door
to lower the boredom, or ring myself

pretending to be a tourist
looking for the best phone in town.

Occasionally some townie
picks up my private calls,

with their friends crowding round,
not one at a time,

urging them to say something witty
like 'Hello'.

People putting advertisements in my windows
without asking, really gets my goat,

sometimes I jam the door and don't let them leave.
Though I have morals like everyone else

but not at two in the morning
when even a phone box needs her sleep.

Myself

The door is a closing mouth. I'm sorry,
but my teeth grind and spark me off,
the sound of my own breathing, the gnawing
of my lip, makes me edgy, angry.
I snore at night and keep myself awake.
Pacing my bedroom like a jailer, red hands
over big ears, does no good. And my god!
The way I eat! It's disgusting,
with my knife ripping and my fork prodding.
Inside my stomach there is warfare,
food writhing in annoyance. I'm getting bigger, blotting
my personal space. Ink spreading across sponge.

The girls took me out in the sunshine, the pavements
shuddered underfoot and the bushes reared away
from the path. Never again. The girls are tactful,
hide their clenched fists, their twitching cheeks.
I hate it and tell them to leave, shut the door.
Muttering sends shivers down my spine.
I tap constantly on tables, drives me up the wall
and onto the roof with the bird shit. Can't talk
to myself any more without interrupting,
shut up shut up shut up, mind your own business.

Middle of the Road

It's the middle of the road.
You found it sort of inviting.
When, as kids, you and your friends
used to sit on the pavement,
playing chicken and remembering to swear,
you used to dare each other to try it,
Go on, go on, the middle of the road,
for a second, just for a second.
All the parents did it when they were kids,
sat in the middle of the road,
in their ripped T-shirts and their dungarees
saying how they were all going to be abstract artists
and never get a nine to five job.
Though there were hardly any cars,
you lived in a safe neighbourhood.

But it's the middle of the road.
And it's all slightly straight and evenly spaced.
Can hardly remember the hard shoulder,
or how to park on a double yellow line.
It's the middle of the road
and you're wearing a uniform,
have to get to work for nine o'clock.
Tucking in your shirt,
yanking down your skirt.
Wouldn't catch you dead in the back of a lorry.
Wouldn't catch you dead with your bum on the curb.
You thought this would just be a stepping stone,
turnstile, money in your pocket,
thought you wouldn't be here for long.

Advertisement for the Lonely Heads Column

Been looking for a body to put my head on,
maybe I could balance mine on yours?
Been looking for temptation but have found none,
been campaigning for my own selfish cause.

Been lonely with just my head for companion,
been having arguments with myself all day,
makes you want to throw it off the tallest building,
makes you want to start a face-free day.

Been looking for a simple body to fall back on,
been looking for something that'll always be there.
Been looking for diamonds in the dustbin,
been looking for thought-waves in the air.

Been looking for a head-less companion
no strings attached, just a pair of shoulders.
I'll send you a picture of myself,
but please reply before I get any older.

Been spinning with no hands to hold my head in,
been trying to keep it all in place,
been bouncing my head against the walls again,
been changing the shape of my face.

But still I can't find anyone who wants it,
I would give it away for an unlimited time.
So if you have an image and want to change it,
then, *catch*, you can borrow mine.

Multitude

An army of you, hiding at the back of my eyes,
on the curve of my iris, trampolining.
I'm loping again down a street
much like the one on the letter.
The one dusting itself at the foot of my bed,
steaming with commas and question marks.
Your road is claustrophobic,
when I reach your house it'll just be a straw
sucked on by sky. I have hands like slaughter,
I have blood on my chest, the left-hand side,
it's flowing like boiling red butter.
I have internal bruises too, just inside my ribs,
just below my shoulder.
I wish your house would puff away in a cloud
of transparent smoke, would leave me standing here
like a pole staring into space.
But it's getting larger with every lope I take.
The dandelions in the garden have your face,
they frown and shake their heads.
Even the dog dirt looks like you.
How come you have such a big door?
Brass handles, padlocks and chains,
an inch of barbed wire over each daffodil,
each flower and weed. I knock, hoping
for some reason, that I might answer the door myself,
and that I might be you, coming to talk it over.

The Earth, the Sky and Molly

God has a wife called Molly,
together they made mankind.
They like to say they're lesbian
for God has a feminine mind.

He once had an affair with Mary,
it didn't last that long,
they had meant to have a girl
but then it all went wrong.

So Molly went off with an angel
and dyed her hair bright pink,
she left a note for God
saying she needed time to think.

But now they're back together,
they cancelled the divorce,
she forces him to go to church
and he cooks of course.

Molly has a husband called God,
they live above us all.
Even though she straps him to a cloud,
he's certain he will fall.

The Radiator in Your Room

I'm thinking of the radiator in your room.
I'm thinking of all your knife-in-the-dark remarks,
of the way you fold yourself into bed like a fig-roll
and blow out the lights with the breath of a switch.

I'm fast forwarding through swirling colours
and tilting handshakes, an agreement sealed by a word,
only a word, only a cheek tongue cough
that came out wrong. I'm rewinding
all my dreams, the way they flow
like a tap of steaming memories through a sieve
of boiling red lights on your digital alarm clock.
I'm pausing flashbacks and printing them out:
they smell of ink and freshly cut trees,
they smell of mornings, lying with my back
to the ceiling, my cooling dreams a puddle on the floor.

I'm thinking of rain drawn back up the ladder
of your tree-house and into the sky, making you
younger by a few seconds. I'm thinking of babies
drinking from troughs of milk, being pigs for a day
and builders with muscles like radishes,
breaking their backs on the final brick.

Friday 13th

Friday 13th, full moon. The girl with the razor-
sharp eyebrow and the downward lip. The boy
with the disjointed nose. I watch,
pick up tricks of the trade
as the beautiful tend their flocks of well-brushed hair,
outnumbered,
lost against the moon and its acne-pocked face.

Unseen

Flailing fingers toward the sky,
a film of rain on your lips.
Falling, faking a truth
as you dance away down the street,
come back walking,
talking too fast.
Twelve trees and a bush
with a view of the sea,
scattering, spraying clouds in puddles of mud.
A jigsaw, seesaw, slide,
water in your eyes,
goodbye to neon lights and park benches,
stretching out of sight.
Blagging a ride on a minibus
stealing a coin for the phone,
dialing tone, waving goodbye
to every sod in town,
who'd leave you to drown in the sunlight.
Smiles like a cynical searchlight,
you can't get away.
Walking on each crack in the pavement,
falling down manholes beneath rolling clouds.
Skies wishing they were compact,
complete, not so vulnerable,
vague and looked up to.
You grin at me,
dancing forward and back,
you look stupid but utterly composed.
How wide is the sky? I ask you.
You reply, larger than the width of your eyes.

Burning and Crashing

Just before he kicked it – the bucket, I mean –
he'd grabbed your gaze like a gun,
held it there, 'You know how much
I love you, don't you?'
You chucked his dying wish
into the nearest bottle-bank,
listened to the smash of his
funny little dreams, instead burnt him up
and threw him about
to show your last respects, the right way.
You keep him in a matchbox now,
safe beneath the sink.

You have no new ways to remember.
Only the ashes to ashes, dirt to disinfectant
and the red wine that you drink
after slicing beetroot on the sideboard.
A simple cut through the heart
of a lettuce brings you to tears.

You remember his orange-juice breath
as he dipped his blueberry eye
into your chocolate one, his only request –
'On the day of my funeral, each of my loved ones
shall be slipped a slice of pie
at the church door, wrapped in velvet,
which they will eat, slowly, slowly,
as the service drones on,
thinking, how tasty, how tasty, how pleasing.
Then – he squeezed your hand here – *picture it…*
the lifting of the lid, the stopping of songs,
to find… no body! No body? Where is he?
He can't have legged it, he's dead as a doorknob!
The tremble of his laugh shook the little white bed.
All that time! Each tender piece of oozing meat
flavoured with thick gravy. I want them all
to enjoy me, to savour every swallow,
I want to live on in the stomachs and skin,
the urine, blood, sweat and beer-bellies.
You know how much I love you, don't you?'

Bonkers.
Out of his tree and roaring like a fool.
You ordered the ambulance like a pizza,
scraped a single hymn across your tongue,
it rained, the coffin was heavy, burning,
then weightless. His face lit up, one last time.

Your frown deepens like a valley now,
but no matter. Years crash like colours
against the sides of the washing machine
and you see his face
in your casseroles, sometimes.

Before the Story Goes

Finally I turned around in the plastic seat,
make-up flaking in the moonlight, to look
until you stopped making sense.
You were writing my name in the air
with your snub nose, injecting your mouth
with gum from a pink packet.
I watched the thought bubbles stretch
and blow themselves up. Funny,
how the night sometimes freezes,
poises me in one of those statue modes,
where however much I try, I can't raise my head.
And so, before the morning when the story goes,
we sat, you and I, on the verge of hating.
Your eyes level with the window, mine
with the crack in the door, becoming smaller
with every flicker of a breath.

Tipping Wine

Something woke me,
I followed the thick stream of carpet,
avoiding creaks and keeping to the side
of the stairs, as if this wasn't
my house. I could hear
the chink of a wine bottle,
I knew it was you.
My bare feet touched the ice
of the tiles, the word 'Cheers' spoken
as if to yourself.
You were sitting in the kitchen,
tipping wine into your mouth
from inches away to tease yourself.
I moved a chair and sat down,
you raised your glass to me.
I asked you to stay,
of course you nodded, but said
you might just go for a walk first.

In Love with the Ice-cream Man

A month ago the serpent came for tea.
He sneered at my salads,
took one lick of my carrot soup
then snapped back his tongue.
He suggested Angel Delight instead of apples,
apples are two-a-penny
and that story's been worn out.
After eyeing my tiny waist
he said, let me tempt you out of Eden
with this creamy eclair.
Now all of a sudden, I'm filling my boots.

I'm finding bits of my body
that I'd misplaced. All that eye-watering
weight-loss, slipping from skins, caving,
carving my cheeks like a fish.
Those flower-buds of flesh, excess fat,
that I'd locked in a box beneath my bed
and would have swallowed the key,
but for the calories.

Now I'm nursing the make-believe baby
in my stomach, smile as it grows again,
I play the bass drum on my thighs
and fumble at the keys of my lips with full fingers.

I am in love with the ice-cream man.
The girl next-door is in love with the butcher.
We have a water-tight plan.

I drip her praises over thick slabs of meat,
play at matchmaking, until he swoops
over with a skinny bunch of flowers
and smothers her in low-fat kisses.
In return she stoppers my mouth
with a mint-choc-chip cone
and shares a dose of her tinkling laugh.

I've stopped being a blade of grass,
now I am a tree. I can hold her hand
tighter than the butcher ever could,
the butcher is a sap. When he sails off
in his spotless apron, I bring out the chocolate.
Like Eve, I pop them one by one
onto her tempted tongue, as the scheming
serpent shimmers
in his wavering scales.

Playing at Families

When you can pick up your mother in thickset hands,
roll her over and tenderly remove her wings.

When you can rip off your father's moustache
with a twitch of finger and thumb,

telling him, 'It'll never do good with the ladies,
not any more.'

When you can place them on your shelf,
like miniature models, knowing that every night

they search the bedroom,
looking for lovers and empty wine bottles,

but melt into the carpet when you open your eyes.
When you can arrange your grandparents in tiny velvet chairs

and gently put them in the embers of the fire,
soothing them through cooing lips

that you're 'Well fed and educated,' so there's no need to worry.
When you can put your relatives in separate boxes

to make sure they don't breed or cut each other's hair
while you're out of the house.

When you can lift them, light as a feather, kiss them
and tuck them in matchbox beds,

making sure your family are locked in innocent slumber,
before leaving to go clubbing every night.

When you can do all this, then you have to face the guilt
when finally, after too many years, you creep back in

to find each wide awake and crying
that they hadn't known where you were.

The Enclosure Act

Apple-bobbing for my reflection in icy water, the same sky
every morning, grey like the colour of the Parson's eyes.
I go to church like a good boy, keep my promises
like a better boy, keep the draught out with a fiery glance.
I lost a copper this morning, it sank into the crops like mud
on brown jackets. The house I live in tilts on the edge
of the hill, it is the end of an up rise and the beginning of a fall,
but it operates by hand. A manual breath blows out the candle
and a manual spade turns the soil until it curdles.
Soil can be soap. Rain can mean summer.

Everything around me is divided by a fine line, the border
my father seesawed on, arrived at heaven just after closing time,
had to wait outside in the dirty star drain.
It's the monster you see, the monster with a thousand hands.
Machines screwing in the nails at the side of your head,
money is time, time is money, life is a filthy copper coin.
Strip it down, seal it up and close it off. The enclosure act,
the promotion of prison, the swinging cage above a sea of barley.
Moved out of the house today, couldn't find my reflection
in the well, the laughter of the rich making the grime swirl.

Going on the town for good. Bright lights, red kisses like slaps
from the landlord's daughter. Over time, with the city
as my fickle friend, I too grow a thousand hands,
I don't wash them every morning. The sky is murky here,
I swear it's a different one. It's not blue or grey,
but black like the eyes of a treacherous dog,
who returns your strokes by ripping out your limbs.

There're no fences in the city, no stroll along paths
that lead to a New Year's day. Lose a penny?
Simply sow another seed. Not in the city. No sweet
country springs that hide in your nostrils to last you out the winter,
here the winter is winter until the cold dawn strikes.
Follow the fine line to the edge of eternity
and it will only bring you back. Take a deep breath,
then a second to smother the taste of the first.

Shadow on My Shoulder

I've got your shadow on my shoulder.
It has its legs around my neck,
I can feel its nails in my hair,
searching for my roots,
searching for my battery.
I try not to stoop though it's heavy.

We walk through the streets, go to the park,
get blurred on the roundabout
and pushed too high on the swings
because we're not kids any more.
I ask it politely when it's planning to move on,
it has a voice like a dialing tone.
You know I'm never gonna leave you.

I bend to tie my laces in a big fat loop.

I have your shadow on my shoulder,
we share our grudges. It strokes my ears
as we catch a falling star and clench both fists,
as we pass a kissing couple
and kick them goodbye.

'Temper, Temper'

Temper, temper,
wherefore art thou temper?
When I should be laughing at your sweet little cries
as I sweep you up in my arms
and chuck you across the room,
as I set your hair alight
and throw you down like a red balloon and stamp on you,
sending you hissing away into the sky.
Instead I'm releasing a series of small sighs
as I smile at you politely, nod
and smile
and nod
and smile
politely.
For after all you are my teacher
and I respect you so very much.

Snake-eyed Smiles

The evening is when I love you most
when your face is like rainfall, or hot snow
and your eyes mist up, mist that my glittering
tongue won't lick clear. When your pupils
are like sequins and you see me through a film
of transparent people with faces nothing like mine.

I love you most when you do your girly thing,
pull me out in the rain and cover me
with pink nail varnish and snake-eyed smiles.
When you hold me, tiptoe through me
like you know me outside in. Smother me
with shampoo, get it in my ears, my nose,
my mouth. Clean me until my eyes slide
in polished sockets, and roll to rest by you.

Lying in wet grass, dew slowly sprouting
in our pores. The has-beens, the should-have-beens,
the love stories. It makes me cringe now
when you speak, makes me want to shut you up
with pillows and duvets and eyelids,
with a tender bump on the head. You can't
chose who you dream of when you sleep.

I talk to you in code. I try to whisper,
I try to spill the *here we go*,
The *I've been wanting to tell you.*
the *chew it over, spit it out and slam it down*,
                       the *I love you.*
I roll my shining tongue but it clings on.
It cowers and shivers in the corner of my cheek,
stage fright, then dives back down,
leaving my mouth like an underwater cave
that big pink boats swerve away from,
thinking there is nothing inside.

Seven Ways of Looking at a Fire

Fiery.

Inhaling the room
and breathing it out
through the chimney.

Kicking and squirming,
as if trying to escape
from a tight black dress.

Underneath, at the belly, glowing
with hidden pride, heat,
removing the night like a waistcoat
and hanging it out to dry.

A burning
black
wigwam
with a yellow hat
and a red umbrella,
opening and closing,
dancing.

From a slant with my eyes
propped up.

Reflected off the floor.

Measurements

'How wide is the sky?' You ask me, bloodshot eyes,
sprawling fingers towards the window, telling me to measure
with the palm of my hand. I smile and put my arm around

your shoulders, I can feel the bones in your back. We both
know I hate it when you ask me this, your eyes placid, daring
me to punch you lightly on the elbow and say 'A million miles.'

You shrug off my arm, instead stroke the arm of the chair.
'Maybe the window stops you seeing it in full,' I whisper
and you fall off your stool, break the window with your fist,

order me to breathe deep. After picking up the glass, you ask me
'How wide is the sky?' holding your hand to my face, covering
the light from the garden. 'That wide,' I say and you smile,
relax your shoulders.

Suddenly I was Hilarious

Even the rain was throwing back its head.
I never knew I was so funny. They were pulling out their hair
in clumps and stuffing it in their mouths, they were sitting
on window-sills and falling out of windows.
I can't quite remember how it started,
maybe when the bedclothes tittered as I headed for the sink
and the toothbrush chattered on my teeth.

When I reached the foot of the stairs,
the girl with the ponytail choked on her own tongue
and the man with the face like a paving slab cracked up.
Suddenly I was hilarious. I was perched cross-legged on the sofa,
the sky collapsing down into the drains,
I had everyone from the neighbourhood gathered
around my ankles, bursting.
I had them all in stitches just by twitching my eye.

But the rain stopped at midnight.

By this time their throats were bleeding
and helicopters had sifted people in from around the globe,
just to catch a glimpse.
But when the rain died there was silence.
Then shaking of heads,
and the stepping back into of planes.
After, it was kind of a shock
when I placed a mug on the table and nobody laughed.

Your Heartbreak

No one else is having your heartbreak.
Your perfect pulsing peach
in scarlet syrup,
your creamy self
pitying.

Not even when the whole world
is stacked like chairs
and you are milky-eyed
with sleep, honey, chocolate,
blues before bedtime.

Right here, where your hand is,
all yours. A beautiful, bleeding,
sprouting red roses,
picked in two halves
from the heartbreak tree,
heartbreak.

It is your prize, you've earned it,
heaved it up
from the wishing well
of your throat,
held its broken body,
treasured it, fed it with tears
the size of cupcakes
and nights like shining spoons.

No one else is having your heartbreak.
Or the way it makes the sound of horses' hooves
if you hold a piece in either hand
and bang it together like a coconut.

Throwing a Party

There were two cups balancing the table top,
a man with a hand stirring the sugar.
There were twelve knocks throwing the host at the door,
four mouths opening, closing a smile, a handshake
wrenching you into the room.
Don't you think flowers are lovely?

There were two shoes tottering back
and forth, and twenty-four eyes on the cheesecake.
There were nine green bottles uncorking in time for a toast,
'To Life' – was the best they could muster.
There were eight stern heads shaking in the hall,
four snarls turning four rosy cheeks.

There was a window hiding the sound
of a drunk, five children killing their Barbie dolls,
ten minds black as tarmac
laying sensible streets.
The beds were made in the usual style,
thick but incredibly cold inside. The sound
of six ghostly laughs and heads hitting pillows,
the spin of uncountable dreams.

You were the first to leave as the morning broke,
two fists on the wheel to steer you away.

Little Red Men

The army of little red men with fishhooks
who attack me whenever you speak
and reel me in. They are everywhere,
in the playground, in the bathroom
with their steel-cut eyes and their horrid smiles.
That time in the park when you became real
for a second and I saw the faces. I saw the quick
red spurts of tongue through sharp red cheeks,
I saw their raised hooks
and the sparks in their mouths,
I watched them as they hammered the park.
I saw the swings mutated, I saw the curving slide
in steady flame, I saw the see-saw flying out to sea.
All the while I was in your system,
fighting with my fists,
rising like a thick black bubble
trying to find the nearest door, an open space
A place where your spinning laugh stood still.

'I came to see if you were OK'

I came to see if you were OK,
not because I'm bothered, but because
my mate asked me to because he
had something to do that probably
could have waited until tomorrow
and all that but he wasn't going to
come anyway but his mum said
or something, but anyway I was
asked to tell you, at least I think
I've remembered it right, that there's
no need to be down and stuff
because we'll always be your friends.
Um... I'm not actually part of that
we because I don't know you.
Anyway you look OK.

Badger Watching

Badger watching wasn't my first choice,
or my second either, but here we are, face down
like playing cards on the brink of a hill.
Stars and molehills, waiting for the badgers.

We'd painted our faces, unravelled
down the lane before the cold could track us down.
But now, now that your voice is seeping into my pores
and the badgers have stood us up, left us at the altar

with a tuft of grass and a tree, it's tempting,
tempting to tilt sideways and leave you behind,
roll hips first down badger mountain
into the blue green belly of the lake.

After two hours we will leave, avoiding the path
because we prefer to trip up, but pretending,
behind our foreheads, that we could have seen badgers.
Maybe, if we'd enticed them out with sausages.

Where the School Ends

OK, so I would follow you home. The sun
dragging at my feet, I remember,
and how puzzled the back of your neck looked
as if you knew I was there.
It was close enough, just to watch your footsteps
disappear as the snow thickened,
just to see the light
seep into the pavement as the night fell down.

It was tempting to catch you up sometimes,
to tread on your heels, instead of dazing
down the corridor and into the street,
a step behind, dancing a slow dance
across the tarmac, moon-walking
the climbing frame and into the mud.
But just where the school ends I forget,
where the beginning stops.

There's so many right words,
I could talk about the glimmer of a face
behind a window and hot chocolate
drunk with a spoon. I could linger on
the tying of a shoelace or the twitch of a lip.
But that doesn't work, best use the wrong words,
the turn of a heel, the tear on the rim
of the sink, the blatant surprise
of a dream that split down the middle.

OK, so I would follow you home.
I'd like to say through the blossom trees
with the sun skimming light across your hair,
but it's more like dark, more like cold,
more like waiting for nothing
as the night crept into my jacket
making me shiver
and want to be somewhere else.

Passing the Time

Thirty paperclip statues on every table in the house
and things are slightly boring without you.
I've knitted a multicoloured jacket for every woodlouse
in the park. But what can you do?

I've given all of the cracks in the pavement pet names
and taken snapshots of individual specks of dust,
though I am not a trainspotter and deny all those claims
but have developed an interest in rust.

The budgies in the petshop now speak fluent French
and I have made friends with a golf commentator.
I was restless one evening so dug a fifty foot trench
then filled it in ten seconds later.

I drank sixty cups of tea in one afternoon
and filled the kettle by collecting drops of dew.
Gardeners' Question Time is on really soon
and things are slightly boring without you.

Close to Home

Someone screamed at the back when the bus
swerved a little close to home,
we'd sold the soles of our shoes to travel
but still no door to poke our heads round.

We passed a dog with the face of a politician
and somewhere in that blue black night
a wolf howled, or not a wolf, maybe
anything breathing. Like the tumour spreading

inside the dead man, we turned the corner
and it was just as we remembered it
but everything was dark and everything was quiet.

I Know this Because You Told Me

I'll break my neck if I jump again from the top of these stairs.
I'll suffer for the rest of my life in hospital
if I put my finger up my nose and then the wind changes.
I know this because you told me.

I'll drown if I jump once more in this nice muddy puddle,
there'll be a flash flood and the rain will rise and take us all.
The world should live in perfect harmony
and you'll kill the bloody neighbours if they don't trim their hedge.

I should never swear, I know this because you told me.
If I talk to the teachers about our mortgage and the fact
that we don't pay our bills, then a monster will come out of the toilet
in the dead of night and pull me down.

You are not joking and only want to warn me. You are a good parent
and tell me life as it is, I know this because you told me.
If I fall in love at seventeen then it will not last.
If I eat too much I will explode and muck up your new shirt.

If I burp then I will blow myself inside out. The world
is quite a strange place and everyone is strange except you.
I know this because you told me.
If I take money from your wallet it is called crime,

if you take money from my piggy bank it is called borrowing.
If I never have a bath I will smell and people won't walk
on the same side of the street as me,
but if I do then I'll be sucked down the plug hole. Some women shave.

I know this because you told me. The banister is for holding,
not for sliding down and you were never rude to your parents.
I will break my neck if I jump again from the top of these stairs
and no, I should not do it anyway.

Bubble Bath

Like shattered glass, we went our different ways,
you across the bridge and down where the traffic was,
me, down an alleyway without an address.
Now, you could pass me in the street. The letter
was frank and without emotion, written on the back
of a napkin while you washed the dishes, typed
with one finger fumbling the keys. That's rich that is,
stroke my hair like I was bubble bath, then brisk home
through the trees, where the fountains run frozen
and the breeze changes the shape of your face.

Gothic

Don't let us near your children.
Attitudes, we'll give you roses for eyes,

smash us half a chance. Though now and then
we get words stuck in our stomachs,
smiles like snakes on our tongues,
but most of the time we're all right.

Full moon on the night, swept in
with our coats like black rivers, scowls
on our sleeves. I almost had you down for dead,
but you chickened out that time.

Rituals done and dusted, pour the blood
into wine, falling behind with the school work,
falling behind with the school,
take a sip of this my dear and show a bit more leg.

Brisk, we don't walk, we roam.
Stir it up until it gets you by the tonsils,
whatever amuses, spur of the shock.
Though now and then we feel a shiver,

tears of salt ice. Full moon on the night,
we'll be fifteen soon. Take our drinks
to the watchtower, witness the sun dissolve
under the murmur of a chant.

Think of your children, as we raise our glasses,
focus our emerald eyes.

Rambling like Ramblers

A tree has fallen asleep with its eyes open, standing up,
and the cracks in the walls are dribbling down the rocks.
The sun is wandering around behind us
as if it's just woken up in the strangest place.
Enough blue sky to make a sailor a massive pair of pants.
We ramble like ramblers, tripping over hills,
not hills, just horizontal fields that have gone wonky.

Gingerbread House

He smelt of 'fresh from the oven' adulthood,
his tongue on the hinge of his lips, his eyes spinning
with sex and cinnamon as he invited you in.
You gazed with wonder at his gingerbread house,
rocking back on your heels with childish delight.
You took a long drag on your lollypop stick
then flicked it away.
Later you spat it all back out to your friends,
showed them the goodies you'd brought back
hidden underneath your tongue. You licked
their pink bedrooms with your knowledge,
spread your laughter thumb-deep on their walls,
tasted the irony on your teeth.

Look little children, come peek at the trail of bread,
look how the teeth marks are still fresh
since they were ripped from the loaf,
look how the birds swoop, hundreds and thousands
of hungry red mouths.

Liquorice doormat, sherbet-coated window pane,
marzipan-stained glass, milk chocolate letterbox,
gingerbread door. His hair like spun sugar
in your hands.
More cream in your coffee dear?
You really are the sweetest child.

Running through the forest, the soft breeze
at each girl's back, like the sound of fairies' wings.
Swooping, diving, disappearing in the shadows,
they come like wolves to the house where he sleeps.
The wizard, the prince, the eldest son
and as his walls are eaten from around his bed,
he dreams of adult things, running, swooping,
diving and of how the sugar doesn't taste as sweet
once you've gorged, indulged, stuffed yourself
with every crumb, every lick and strip.
Left not a single melting piece untouched.
He smelt of 'fresh from the oven' adulthood
They eat him too, his pale skin vibrates in their fingers,
and the rain falls on his mattress and the place
where his house used to be.

At last, licking their lips they return to the forest,
no longer wolves, just girls. They look for their path
through the night. Lost. They blame the Robins,
they blame the Swallows, they blame the Swans,
the Eagles, they blame the Vultures
and their hungry red mouths.

it only makes me louder. You pass me a thought wave,
I throw it back and we play catch for a while. The winter

is turning slowly back to winter again and I swear
your mouth has changed since I last saw you.

You're withering away in my head, like fresh trees walking
and talking until they realize they can't. The only change

I can deal with is the curve between blue eyes and sleep,
my guitar looks like a machine gun if I squint slightly

and the wind picks up another draughty hand, waves it
around a bit until it thinks we're all watching,

then spits in our eyes. I can vaguely remember
vaguely remembering a look you gave me,

or it might just be a photo or a tear. A dreary cardigan-faced
doctor once told me that I'd grow up into my mum,

like an apple seed that grows inside your stomach
until you can reach in and pick out fruit from your oesophagus.

Silence doesn't bother me it only makes me slower,
as winter turns swiftly into winter,

pass me another aspirin and I'll dissolve.

A Piece of Stained Glass in a Lonely Church

I hate the way they see right through me,
beyond my dark tinted humour, beyond
the fact that I am the glass of a Saint's eye.

They can tell I'm not religious. A rebellious
little snippet of a window, trapped between
transparent friends. Forced to eat, sleep

and drink these walls, opaque, big old Christian bricks.
Happy days, eyeing up children with stones,
hoping they'll chuck them. But what I want to know is:

will I go to hell for wishing
to be soundproof,
double glazed?

At the Mention of Rain

At the mention of rain, they moved all the furniture
upstairs. We thought it strange, from our turret,
perched on the climbing frame
where the birds didn't dare shit, our names
scrawled in biro on the wood. Couldn't stomach
organized folk, making sure they'd pockets with zips
and five bolts on their doors.

At the mention of rain, we forgot umbrellas, coats,
jumpers, loped about in puddles, getting wet.
Hot blooded, to prove it Craig took off his T-shirt,
went slightly purple but lived to brag the tale,
didn't need a bath that night.

At the mention of rain, those silly tossers in number 38
built an ark, went around collecting planks of wood
from various tree-houses. We perched on our turret, sneering.
Then it began chucking it down, raindrops big as your fist,
we laughed and opened our mouths.
Didn't know the climbing frame could float.

Craig took off his trousers for a bet
and caught pneumonia. Hot blooded? That's a joke.
At the mention of rain they brought the whole
of London zoo down the high street, bet they had locks
on every room in that bloody ark. I won the bet,
but Craig died (conveniently) before he could pay up.

But the frame's almost gone now,
me and the gang watched them sail away, nice and dry,
bet they thought they were so clever.
Glug, drank some of the water, salty,
too much will give me heart trouble. *Glug*.
Or on the other hand, I could drown.

But a damn respectable death, going down
with the ship, climbing frame, whatever. A dove
just shat on my head. That's it, the last, *glug*, straw,
glug, bloody, *glug glug*, 38, *glug*, at the mention of rain.

Geography Lessons

When you've reached the peak,
the summit, the end,
you've come to the limit,
let me tell you gently
that the world is round, my sweet,
and it's all a long walk backwards,
starting from here.

Serious Living

The house is quieter than a sedated mouse,
outside the sun rains pineapple chunks
and I'm all on my lonesome
with only so much that biscuits can do.

I'm over the loss of my mate next-door,
moving house a year ago without telling me
and I've come to accept that the vet
can never mend our dog,
but ever since you mentioned, with tact,
that I really had to start living,
you've somehow made me stop.

I've never played scrabble with the queen.
And the deliberate tilting, then dropping,
of strangers on the dance floor
seems to have passed me by.
I've never fainted on the spot,
or annoyingly ruffled your hair.
Still have yet to shrug, half smile
and say 'It's not me, it's you,'
to strut, restrain a backwards glance.
Never tottered, drunk on high-heels,
into a fountain. Never had an occasion rise to me.

So why, when it came to the crunch,
did I always apple crumble? Why the niggling?
The gnawing, never forgetting, regretting never
thickly spreading jam on your T.V.,
shaving my name into your cat,
dragging you out into the moonlight
to be violently sick on your shoes?

The house is quieter than a sedated mouse.
You used to boast that you would be the first
to make a worm cry, the first to moon-walk Everest.
You swore you once fell asleep with a snake
around your neck. You claimed to have girlfriends
in every country of the world.

I am leaving the house and heading for the coast.
Just you watch and call this living. Beat this. Top this.
For tonight, my dear, without a helmet,
I will launch out, amidst thunder and lightning,
into the ocean, on a raft made out of sponge
and become the first to take the storm by storm.

My Love

I like you best when you're not here, my love.
Flowers are colourful knives, smiles, frowns
plastered in foundation, blaming eyes simply
pools of affection. My love. Don't relax, don't sit back.
The ghosts who have finished their business,
but hang around purely for fun, rustle the curtains
in the morning and put salt in my mouth as I sleep.
I wake with grains of hate on my tongue.
My love, for you are the source of the winding
sewers, the bursting balloon pumped with spite
that shatters into the sky. If I throw you off
it will rise even higher, darling. Outside car doors
are slamming, alarms are being triggered, people
run like blurs across blank pages that are soon
to be filled. I like you best when you're not here,
my love. No, I won't get up, you can let yourself out.

Too Late for Breakfast

There is a blue paper star above the window, shimmering dust.
It is early, too early for lunch, but too late for breakfast.
The colours in this room have faded overnight like stains
that have almost been cleaned. The sound of birds
singing backwards through the trees.
The curtains are closed.

A woman is collecting her scarf from the feet of a man,
preparing to go. She has jewels in her hair that fall out
when she shakes it and she keeps her hands naked of rings, always.
Move to the right and there is a box which won't shut,
crammed to the brim with dresses and presents,
that people she has forgotten once gave her.

Backwards

The balcony didn't take sides.

Your smooth cold hand, the night tempting and intriguing
like the soft words of a sleepwalker.
Fists unclenched from the railings, the wind on our tongues.

I can still see our intake of breath, weeks later, frozen on the air,
still feel the impact of love on my face
as we hit the ground. The balcony kept its mouth shut.

Dropped us both, like hearts sliding down from throats.
It claimed to see nothing, but leant to watch us slip away.
Me and you, and this darkness in between, sullen,

so hard to make sense. Easier to reverse, take it by the last thread
and yank until everything is undone. Simple. Beginning with goodbye
and your car raging back into the drive.

Knowing that you are going nowhere soon, I can moon-walk
the stairs and sink face-forward into bed with the fading smell
of future sweat. My dreams untangle into last night,

I wake into the evening with your name on my skin.
My bruises darken. Eleven thirty, behind my door, thoughts
erupt and erase until ten when I return to the dining room

to throw up food neatly onto a shining plate. I light
the fire with dead matches as something that was broken
becomes whole again and you storm in to withdraw

your apology. Say that you're about to storm out.
But this time you don't. Instead lead me by the thumb
into the moonlight, where our tears run dry over the daffodils.

Then a silence, backwards or not, a slice of peace
before I am slammed to the ground. You wake me,
press my eyelids down, crush me into the gravel

and lie down beside. The strange sound of music
is drawn into a distant window. Slowly your arm
flinches from my shoulder as my face ripples and heals,

rises from the ground. Our hearts lift to touch our tongues,
until we're back on the balcony with our whole lives behind us.
Moments black-hole themselves. We forget how to fly.

Lean away from the railings, black eyes become blue
and uttered words push like thick gold coins between our lips,
suddenly unspoken.

Taking Me Down

I'm down the sofa, curling at the ears,
lodged in a book you gave up on.
There are no dark patches to prove
I was there, swinging on hooks
between cheap frames. Me with my tongue out,
me with your candy-floss fists
around my waist, as we shot
like new-borns from the helter-skelter.
Me with your cat at arm's length.
You didn't even save the morning,
the crushes, dance music, hidden
chocolate licked from our hands,
when we crept into every bedroom
to smear salad cream on their faces as they slept,
watched them wrinkle their freckled noses
and bury their heads, until it spread
like a pale disease. The pictures we took then.
Not even the snapshot of my throbbing bump
after you punched me in the head
reaching for the alarm clock. Now it's stopped
being one big sleep-over.

You're busy this weekend. If there was a party
would you tell me? I am always invited, any time,
but you can't guarantee you'll be in.

Entirely

And it was entirely the words that I mumbled in the second
between looking at the carpet and looking at you.
And it was clearly the drink to my lips
and the whisper of my feet through the air as I tackled
the door to the ground and leapt on the phone.
And it was completely the fact that it was a wrong number
and the stain down my jacket and the empty coke can.
And it was mainly the glances
and the poems and the cigarette lighters.
And it was totally the chewing gum stuck to my windpipe
when you remembered my name
and then helped with turning me upside down
and thumping me on the chest until I stopped choking.
But most of all it was the rain and the crossleggedness
of us on the sofa with a slim chance of conversation
and a syllable to last us the night.

Toothpaste

I dreamt I stumbled out of sleep and onto the tiles
and you turned the key and my eyes were open,
you brought a homely feeling with you and scattered
my family into your swag bag and took all the toothpaste,
the keyhole leaving moonshine on my face,
I dreamt you left a calling card in the letterbox

The postman stepped in through the letterbox
the next morning, and the bath chucked water on the tiles.
The mirror snarled with dreams of ugly faces
and the wind poured in like treacle from the open
window, you were sleeping, you were scattered
on the bed, the sink was ankle-deep in toothpaste.

I burnt the kettle dry, you woke with scattered
wrinkles as if you'd slept all night with holly on your face.
I kissed you good morning and you handed me the toothpaste.
When I went into the sunshine, I squashed the cat into a tile,
I don't have a cat. The people, who were neighbours, opened
and closed their doors as I passed and looked through their
                                            letterboxes.

There was a tear on the newsagent counter crying without a face
and assistants scattered from the roof to hand me my toothpaste
like always, though I never ask for change. The door was open,
I stepped right out into a man with a face like a letterbox
with an eye poking through. The pavement was cement tiles
and probably had children underneath, stony, smiling, scattered.

My family always said that they were lost without toothpaste,
and pearly teeth were like a slice of light in the face.
I danced back to the house and saw you packing on the tiles,
you were taking my home with you and my eyes were scattered
in the photos on the walls. Even the Victorian letterbox
couldn't talk you into staying. All the cupboards were open.

I dreamt I went back to my bed and my eyes were open
and I no longer felt part of anything, the bed clothes were scattered.
I dreamt the calling card that you'd slipped in the letterbox
read: You're lost because I've taken all the toothpaste.
And homely toothpaste tears streamed down my face.
I dreamt in your hurry to leave that you'd cracked all the tiles.

I woke, the night was scattered on my face
and I had splinters of tiles on my feet. I must have looked like a
                                                                letterbox,
open, gaping, and every toothbrush stark naked without you.

I Have Eaten Your Parrot

I have killed your parrot and eaten him.
I am so sorry. I don't know what came over me.
How I could maim and scoff such a nice parrot
that would tell me to 'sod off and die'
whenever I walked in the room? He tasted of chicken.
I'm sorry.

Year of the Woman

It was the year of the woman. You broke a bough
when you sat on a swing, nail varnish on the sides
of your baby doll mouth. Cursed an empty room.

Years at school taught you how to hide your gum
at the top of your mouth. A teacher opened a book
on page forty-nine for a decade. Oh the silence

when you sat down for class and found her gazing
with horror at middle age. Sexy clothes that bit
your bum, tired of hot chocolate, gulped an espresso

without making a face and felt like God.
Backwards and forwards went the clock as you
twizzled in bed with dreams of seedless oranges,

little fingers tapping in time to the car radio
and whipping out a twenty pound note just to listen
to the sound. It was the year of the woman.

You had the backhand sulk, the nonchalance,
the eyebrow, even the 'just had a bath and passed
all my exams' grammar school lark, all to perfection.

But you took it all in time, walked with a step
in your dance, a forecast for lighting,
a storm on your tongue
and a bubble in your throat just itching to burst.